MOVIE ★ ICONS

BERGMAN

EDITOR
PAUL DUNCAN

TEXT
SCOTT EYMAN

PHOTOS
THE KOBAL COLLECTION

TASCHEN

HONG KONG KÖLN LONDON LOS ANGELES MADRID PARIS TOKYO

CONTENTS

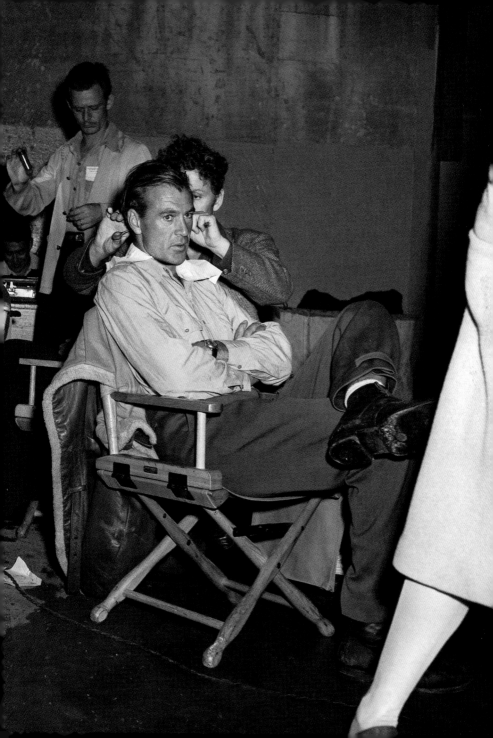

1

INGRID BERGMAN: DREAM GIRL

BY SCOTT EYMAN

TRAUMFRAU

L'IDÉAL FÉMININ

INGRID BERGMAN: DREAM GIRL

by Scott Eyman

Ingrid Bergman was born beautiful, but, unusually for one so blessed, she knew that beauty is never enough. She wanted to be great as well.

Did any movie star of the classic era demonstrate more ambition? On the stage, she performed Strindberg, Ibsen, Turgenev, Shaw, and O'Neill – some several times. On television she acted in Zweig, Henry James, and Cocteau, and in movies there was *Joan of Arc* (1948) and a relentless film for Ingmar Bergman, *Autumn Sonata* (1978).

Those stage performances were acclaimed in their time, but they are gone. What is left is a succession of films recording an indelible combination of profoundly female beauty with stolid peasant strength – a tawny sensuality that made her particularly adept at portraying capitulation to desire.

No leading lady ever melted into her leading men more convincingly, yet Bergman never seemed to be fully emotionally involved with any of her three husbands. She needed romance more than she believed in love, which is why she had affairs with so many strongly masculine men: Gary Cooper, Victor Fleming, Robert Capa, Yul Brynner, and Anthony Quinn.

Orphaned at the age of 12, she transferred the child's need for parental security to her profession. The film set – the warming lights, the easy camaraderie of the crew, the affectionate regard of her fellow actors – was always more meaningful, more rewarding than real life.

Her on-screen emotional dynamic was a canny inversion of the normal pattern. From Miriam Hopkins to Katharine Hepburn to Bette Davis, the preferred method was to establish the actress as a strong-willed woman with a personality of her own who is gradually softened and seduced by the devastating charms of the leading man and the demands of the plot.

"I have no regrets. I wouldn't have lived my life the way I did if I was going to worry about what people were going to say."
Ingrid Bergman

PORTRAIT (1945)

By contrast, from her first American film, *Intermezzo* (1939), to *For Whom the Bell Tolls* (1943) and *Gaslight* (1944) all the way through to *Indiscreet* (1958), Bergman fell in love easily. It was only through the dramatic experiences of the film – and the tribulations of romance and sex – that she found her true self and gained the dramatic weight that enabled her to survive betrayal, mendacity, and even the possibility of death.

The parabola of the American career that followed her incubation as an ingénue in Sweden is remarkable: 11 consecutive successes, including some of the most famous films of the American cinema: *Intermezzo* (1939), *Adam Had Four Sons* (1941), *Rage in Heaven* (1941), *Dr. Jekyll and Mr. Hyde* (1941), *Casablanca* (1942), *For Whom the Bell Tolls* (1943), *Gaslight* (1944), *Saratoga Trunk* (1945), *The Bells of St. Mary's* (1945), *Spellbound* (1945), and *Notorious* (1946).

This unparalleled run of hits was followed by a succession of ignominious commercial and critical failures (*Arch of Triumph* (1948), *Joan of Arc*, *Under Capricorn* (1949), *Stromboli* (1950)) that culminated in an illegitimate pregnancy by her future husband, director Roberto Rossellini. The result was an exile that included several moving if overtly uncommercial movies for Rossellini that uncannily prefigured the existential angst of Michelangelo Antonioni. This period was followed by the extraordinary comeback kicked off by *Anastasia* (1956) that continued, with very few *longueurs*, to the end of her life.

Ultimately, most movies remain locked in their period, even if the personality of the star manages to transcend that period. It is only the greatest stars who achieve those half-dozen or so films that remain perpetually seductive, films that render them, in effect, immortal: *Casablanca*, *Gaslight*, *Spellbound*, *Notorious*, *Journey to Italy* (1954), *Indiscreet*, *Autumn Sonata*.

Ingrid Bergman died in 1982.

Ingrid Bergman lives.

ENDPAPERS/VORSATZBLATT/PAGE DE GARDE
PORTRAIT (1938)

PAGES 2/3
PORTRAIT FOR 'ONLY ONE NIGHT' ('EN ENDA NATT', 1939)

PAGE 4
PORTRAIT (1941)

PAGES 6/7
ON THE SET OF 'FOR WHOM THE BELL TOLLS' (1943)

PAGE 8
PORTRAIT FOR 'SPELLBOUND' (1945)

OPPOSITE/RECHTS/CI-CONTRE
PORTRAIT FOR 'SARATOGA TRUNK' (1945)

INGRID BERGMAN: TRAUMFRAU

von Scott Eyman

Ingrid Bergman war von Natur aus schön, doch im Unterschied zu vielen anderen wusste sie, dass Schönheit allein nicht genug sein kann. Sie strebte nach wahrer Größe.

Welch anderer Filmstar der klassischen Ära bewies mehr Ehrgeiz als sie? Auf der Bühne trat sie – mehrfach – in Stücken von Strindberg, Ibsen, Turgenjew, Shaw und O'Neill auf. Im Fernsehen war sie in Verfilmungen von Werken von Zweig, Henry James und Cocteau zu sehen, und im Kino spielte sie in Andersons *Johanna von Orléans* (1948) und in dem schonungslosen Film *Herbstsonate* (1978) von Ingmar Bergman.

Wurde sie im Theater von ihren Zeitgenossen bejubelt, so gehören diese Auftritte doch unwiederbringlich der Vergangenheit an. Was blieb, war eine Reihe von Filmen, die ihre tiefgründige Schönheit gepaart mit bäuerlicher Sturheit bannten – jene eigenwillige Sinnlichkeit prädestinierte Bergmann insbesondere für Rollen, in denen sie vor dem Begehren kapitulierte.

Keine Hauptdarstellerin schmolz jemals überzeugender in den Armen ihrer männlichen Filmpartner dahin, und doch vermisste man bei Bergman eine enge Gefühlsbindung an alle drei Ehemänner. Sie brauchte die romantische Liebelei mehr, als dass sie an die große Liebe glaubte. Aus diesem Grunde hatte sie Affären mit so maskulinen Männern wie Gary Cooper, Victor Fleming, Robert Capa, Yul Brynner oder Anthony Quinn.

Schon mit zwölf wurde sie Waise, und ihr kindliches Bedürfnis nach elterlicher Fürsorge übertrug die Schauspielerin dann auf ihren Beruf. Die Atmosphäre im Filmstudio – die warmen Leuchten, der kameradschaftliche Umgang im Team, die Wertschätzung ihrer Kollegen –, all dies war ihr stets wichtiger und wertvoller als das Leben außerhalb des Studios.

Ihre emotionale Dynamik auf der Leinwand war eine geschickte Umkehrung des herkömmlichen Musters. Von Miriam Hopkins über Katharine Hepburn bis zu Bette Davis wurden Frauen bevorzugt als willensstarke und eigenständige Persönlichkeiten dargestellt, die sich

PORTRAIT (1939)

„Ich bedaure nichts. Ich hätte mein Leben nicht so gelebt, wie ich es tat, wenn ich mir über das Gerede der Leute Gedanken gemacht hätte."
Ingrid Bergman

vom umwerfenden Charme des männlichen Hauptdarstellers allmählich erweichen und verführen lassen, ganz wie es die Handlung erforderte.

Im Gegensatz dazu waren die Frauen, die Bergman spielte, leichte Beute – von ihrem ersten amerikanischen Film *Intermezzo* (1939) über *Wem die Stunde schlägt* (1943) und *Das Haus der Lady Alquist* (1944) bis hin zu *Indiskret* (1958). Erst durch leidvolle Erfahrungen – auch mit Liebe und Sex – finden die Frauen schließlich zu sich selbst und gewinnen eine innere Stärke, dank derer sie Lügen, Verrat und sogar tödlichen Gefahren trotzen.

An Ingrid Bergmans schwedische Lehrjahre als Naive schloss sich eine beachtliche Karriere in den USA an: Sie drehte elf Erfolgsfilme hintereinander, darunter einige der berühmtesten Filme des amerikanischen Kinos: *Intermezzo* (1939), *Adam hat vier Söhne* (1941), *Gefährliche Liebe* (1941), *Arzt und Dämon* (1941), *Casablanca* (1942), *Wem die Stunde schlägt* (1943), *Das Haus der Lady Alquist* (1944), *Spiel mit dem Schicksal* (aka *Die Intrigantin von Saratoga/ Abrechnung in Saratoga*, 1945), *Die Glocken von St. Marien* (1945), *Ich kämpfe um dich* (1945) und *Berüchtigt* (aka *Weißes Gift*, 1946).

Auf diese beispiellose Erfolgsserie folgten mehrere Flops, die beim Publikum wie auch bei der Kritik durchfielen: *Triumphbogen* (1948), *Johanna von Orléans* (1948), *Sklavin des Herzens* (1949), *Stromboli* (1950). Den „Gipfel" stellte dann die Schwangerschaft infolge ihrer außerehelichen Beziehung zu dem Regisseur Roberto Rossellini dar, den sie später heiratete. Ergebnis war ein Leben im Exil. Zusammen mit Rossellini drehte Ingrid Bergman mehrere bewegende Filme, die ganz offenkundig nicht auf das Massenpublikum zugeschnitten waren, sondern die Existenzangst eines Michelangelo Antonioni vorwegnahmen. Mit *Anastasia* (1956) beginnend, folgte ein außergewöhnliches Comeback, das – von einigen wenigen Durchhängern abgesehen – bis zum Ende ihres Lebens fortdauerte.

Letztlich bleiben Filme meist ihrer Entstehungszeit verhaftet, selbst wenn die Persönlichkeit eines Stars über diese Zeit hinaus zu wirken vermag. Nur den allergrößten Stars gelingt es in vielleicht einem halben Dutzend Filmen, das Publikum dauerhaft in den Bann zu ziehen und damit wahrhaft unsterblich zu werden: *Casablanca*, *Das Haus der Lady Alquist*, *Ich kämpfe um dich*, *Berüchtigt* (aka *Weißes Gift*), *Reise in Italien* (aka *Liebe ist stärker*, 1954), *Indiskret*, *Herbstsonate*.

Ingrid Bergman starb 1982.

Ingrid Bergman lebt.

INGRID BERGMAN : L'IDÉAL FÉMININ

Scott Eyman

Ingrid Bergman est née belle, mais bien que bénie des dieux, elle sait que la beauté ne suffit pas. Elle veut être une grande actrice.

Vit-on jamais star de l'âge d'or du cinéma faire preuve d'autant d'ambition ? Au théâtre, elle interprète Strindberg, Ibsen, Tourgueniev, Shaw et O'Neill. À la télévision, elle apparaît dans des productions tirées de Zweig, Henry James et Cocteau. Au cinéma, elle incarne *Jeanne d'Arc* (1948) et joue dans l'un des films les plus exigeants d'Ingmar Bergman, *Sonate d'automne* (1978).

Bien qu'acclamées en leur temps, ses prestations théâtrales sont hélas perdues pour la postérité. Reste une succession de films témoignant de manière indélébile de sa beauté si féminine alliée à une solide rusticité, qui lui confère une sensualité naïve et la rend particulièrement apte à exprimer la capitulation face au désir.

Jamais actrice ne s'est fondue dans son partenaire avec autant de sincérité. Et pourtant, Ingrid Bergman semble ne s'être réellement donnée à aucun de ses trois époux. Elle a besoin de romantisme sans réellement croire à l'amour, ce qui explique ses nombreuses liaisons avec des hommes pétris de virilité : Gary Cooper, Victor Fleming, Robert Capa, Yul Brynner ou encore Anthony Quinn.

Orpheline à l'âge de 12 ans, elle trouve dans son métier le sentiment de sécurité que ses parents n'ont pu lui donner. Avec la chaleur des projecteurs, la franche camaraderie des techniciens et le regard affectueux de ses partenaires, les plateaux de tournage lui offrent un univers plus épanouissant et plus réconfortant que la vraie vie.

La dynamique émotionnelle qu'elle incarne à l'écran est une habile inversion du schéma habituel. De Miriam Hopkins à Katharine Hepburn en passant par Bette Davis, l'actrice est généralement présentée comme une femme énergique dotée d'une forte personnalité, qui se laisse

PORTRAIT FOR 'SPELLBOUND' (1945)

« Je n'ai aucun regret. Je n'aurais pas vécu comme je l'ai fait si je me souciais du qu'en-dira-t-on. »
Ingrid Bergman

peu à peu attendrir et séduire par le charme dévastateur de son partenaire et les nécessités de l'intrigue.

Inversement, d'*Intermezzo* (son premier film américain, en 1939) à *Indiscret* (1958) en passant par *Pour qui sonne le glas* (1943) et *Hantise* (1944), Ingrid Bergman ne se fait jamais prier pour tomber amoureuse. Ce sont les expériences dramatiques qu'elle endure au cours du film – et les tribulations de sa vie sentimentale et sexuelle – qui lui permettent de découvrir sa véritable identité et d'acquérir la force de survivre à la trahison, au mensonge, voire à la confrontation avec la mort.

À sa période de maturation dans des rôles d'ingénue pour le cinéma suédois succède une carrière américaine à la trajectoire fulgurante : 11 succès consécutifs, dont certains des films les plus célèbres de l'histoire du cinéma : *Intermezzo* (1939), *La Famille Stoddard* (1941), *La Proie du mort* (1941), *Dr. Jekyll et Mr. Hyde* (1941), *Casablanca* (1942), *Pour qui sonne le glas* (1943), *Hantise* (1944), *L'Intrigante de Saratoga* (1945), *Les Cloches de Sainte-Marie* (1945), *La Maison du docteur Edwardes* (1945) et *Les Enchaînés* (1946).

Cet enchaînement de succès sans précédent sera suivi d'une série de douloureux échecs critiques et commerciaux (*Arc de triomphe* [1948], *Jeanne d'Arc*, *Les Amants du Capricorne* [1949], *Stromboli* [1950]). Celle-ci s'achève avec l'annonce de sa grossesse illégitime et de sa liaison avec le réalisateur Roberto Rossellini, qu'elle finira par épouser. Il s'ensuit un exil en Italie durant lequel elle tourne avec Rossellini plusieurs films résolument non commerciaux, qui préfigurent étrangement l'angoisse existentielle de Michelangelo Antonioni. À cette période succède un extraordinaire come-back amorcé par *Anastasia* (1956) et qui se poursuivra, avec quelques rares temps morts, jusqu'à la fin de sa vie.

Avec le recul, la plupart des films demeurent ancrés dans leur époque, même si la personnalité de l'interprète arrive à la transcender. Seules les plus grandes stars parviennent à tourner une demi-douzaine de ces films sur lesquels le temps n'a pas de prise, de ces films qui rendent ces stars immortelles : *Casablanca*, *Hantise*, *La Maison du docteur Edwardes*, *Les Enchaînés*, *Voyage en Italie* (1954), *Indiscret*, *Sonate d'automne*.

Ingrid Bergman s'est éteinte le 29 août 1982.

Ingrid Bergman vit toujours.

MOVIE STORY

SEPTEMBER
15c

Exclusive!

NOTORIOUS

Starring

CARY GRANT and INGRID BERGMAN

2

VISUAL
FILMOGRAPHY

FILMOGRAFIE IN BILDERN
FILMOGRAPHIE EN IMAGES

SWEDEN

SCHWEDEN

LA SUÈDE

**STILL FROM 'OCEAN BREAKERS'
('BRÄNNINGAR', 1935)**
With Weyler Hildeband, in a scene that eerily prefigures
the dynamics of Ingmar Bergman. / Mit Weyler
Hildeband in einer Szene, die auf gespenstische Weise
die Dynamik Ingmar Bergmans vorausahnen lässt. /
Avec Weyler Hildeband dans une scène qui préfigure
étrangement l'œuvre d'Ingmar Bergman.

**STILL FROM 'THE COUNT OF THE MONK'S
BRIDGE' ('MUNKBROGREVEN', 1934)**
The star aged 20, in chrysalis form, cheekbones hidden
behind baby fat. / Mit 20 befand sich der Star noch im
Larvenstadium, und die Wangenknochen verbargen
sich unter Babyspeck. / Ingrid à 20 ans, chrysalide aux
pommettes encore enrobées dans des rondeurs
enfantines.

**STILL FROM 'OCEAN BREAKERS'
('BRÄNNINGAR', 1935)**
With Sten Lindgren, the first of many older men who
would melt Bergman's reserve. / Mit Sten Lindgren,
dem ersten von vielen älteren Männern, die Bergmans
Zurückhaltung zum Schmelzen brachten. / Avec Sten
Lindgren, le premier d'une série d'hommes mûrs qui
auront raison de sa réserve.

*"While [Bergman] has too much the appearance of
a country girl, she is very natural, and is the type
that does not use make-up on her face or on her
mind."*
**Judge at her audition for the Royal Dramatic Theater in
Stockholm**

**STILL FROM 'OCEAN BREAKERS'
('BRÄNNINGAR', 1935)**

„Obwohl [Bergman] zu sehr wie ein Mädchen vom Lande erscheint, ist sie doch sehr natürlich und der Typ, der weder im Gesicht noch im Gemüt eine Maske trägt."
Juror bei ihrem Vorsprechen am Kungliga Dramatiska Teatern in Stockholm

« Bien que [Ingrid Bergman] ait une allure trop paysanne, elle possède un grand naturel ; c'est le genre d'actrice qui ne maquille ni son visage, ni son âme. »
Un membre du jury lors de son audition au Théâtre royal dramatique de Stockholm

**STILL FROM 'THE FAMILY SWEDENHIELMS'
('SWEDENHIELMS', 1935)**
Radiating a perfect, if slightly processed Scandinavian
beauty, opposite Gösta Ekman. / Hier strahlt sie eine
vollkommene, wenn auch leicht gekünstelte skandina-
vische Schönheit aus – mit Gösta Ekman. / D'une beauté
nordique rayonnante, bien qu'un peu artificielle, aux
côtés de Gösta Ekman.

**STILL FROM 'THE FAMILY SWEDENHIELMS'
('SWEDENHIELMS', 1935)**
With Björn Berglund. / Mit Björn Berglund. / Aux côtés
de Björn Berglund.

ON THE SET OF 'WALPURGIS NIGHT'
('VALBORGSMÄSSOAFTON', 1935)
With the great Victor Sjöström (left), who, along with
Mauritz Stiller, defined early Swedish cinema. / Mit dem
großen Victor Sjöström (links), der – gemeinsam mit
Mauritz Stiller – das frühe schwedische Kino prägte. /
Avec le grand Victor Sjöström (à gauche), qui, tout
comme Mauritz Stiller, a marqué les débuts du cinéma
suédois.

PAGES 32/33
STILL FROM 'ON THE SUNNY SIDE'
('PÅ SOLSIDAN', 1936)
One star on her way to Hollywood, one star (Lars
Hanson) happy to be home. / Ein Star auf dem Weg
nach Hollywood, ein anderer Star (Lars Hanson) freut
sich, wieder zu Hause zu sein. / Une star sur le chemin
de Hollywood, une autre (Lars Hanson) de retour au
bercail.

STILL FROM 'WALPURGIS NIGHT'
('VALBORGSMÄSSOAFTON', 1935)
The process of idealizing Bergman was underway
from the beginning. / Von Anfang an wurde Bergman
idealisiert. / Le processus d'idéalisation d'Ingrid
Bergman est déjà en marche.

STILL FROM 'INTERMEZZO' (1936)
With Gösta Ekman in the original May-September
love story. / Mit Gösta Ekman in der ersten Fassung
der Liebesgeschichte zwischen einer jungen Frau und
einem älteren Mann. / Avec Gösta Ekman dans la
première mouture de cette histoire d'amour illicite.

"It's not whether you really cry. It's whether the
audience thinks you are crying."
Ingrid Bergman

„Es geht nicht darum, dass man wirklich weint,
sondern dass das Publikum glaubt, man weine."
Ingrid Bergman

« La question n'est pas de savoir si vous pleurez
vraiment. Le tout est de le faire croire au public. »
Ingrid Bergman

STILL FROM 'INTERMEZZO' (1936)
The anguish of the wife and children while the husband
dallies with his young mistress. / Die Not der Mutter,
während sich der Ehemann und Vater mit seiner jungen
Geliebten vergnügt. / Le mari néglige sa femme et ses
enfants pour se consacrer à sa jeune maîtresse.

PAGES 36/37
PORTRAIT FOR 'INTERMEZZO' (1936)
A heavily made-up look compared to the more natural
presence of Bergman's American films. / Im Gegensatz
zu dem natürlicheren Erscheinungsbild in ihren amerikanischen Filmen ist Bergman hier stark geschminkt. /
Un visage beaucoup plus fardé que dans ses films
américains.

STILL FROM 'DOLLAR' (1938)
Still lending her beauty to comparatively sexless older men. / Wieder gibt sie ihre Schönheit für vergleichsweise unerotische ältere Männer her. / Ingrid continue de prêter sa beauté à des hommes plus âgés et relativement asexués.

"Men make women helpless by deciding and telling them what to do. Men in my life taught me to be dependent, beginning with my father, and after that Uncle Otto, who didn't want me to become an actress, and then Petter, even before our engagement."
Ingrid Bergman

„Männer machen Frauen hilflos, indem sie Entscheidungen treffen und ihnen sagen, was sie zu tun haben. Die Männer in meinem Leben lehrten mich Abhängigkeit, angefangen bei meinem Vater und danach Onkel Otto, der nicht wollte, dass ich Schauspielerin wurde, und dann Petter, noch bevor wir uns verlobten."
Ingrid Bergman

STILL FROM 'DOLLAR' (1938)
Nearly unrecognizable behind period make-up and
clothes. / In Kostüm und Maske im Stil der Epoche ist
sie kaum wiederzuerkennen. / Presque méconnaissable
dans les vêtements et le maquillage d'époque.

« Les hommes rendent les femmes impuissantes
en leur disant ce qu'elles doivent faire. Les hommes
m'ont toujours appris à être dépendante,
à commencer par mon père, puis mon oncle Otto,
qui ne voulait pas que je devienne actrice, puis
Petter, même avant nos fiançailles. »
Ingrid Bergman

STILL FROM 'DOLLAR' (1938)
Part of the ensemble, but inexorably drawing the eye nevertheless. / Obwohl sie in einem Ensemble spielt, zieht sie unweigerlich die Blicke auf sich. / Bien que noyée dans le tableau d'ensemble, elle attire irrésistiblement le regard.

PORTRAIT FOR 'DOLLAR' (1938)
A frank, almost appraisingly sensual look of the sort she would rarely indulge in later. / Ein offener, fast abschätzend sinnlicher Blick jener Art, wie man ihn in späteren Jahren selten bei ihr sah. / Un regard franc, d'une sensualité presque inquisitrice, qu'elle s'autorisera rarement par la suite.

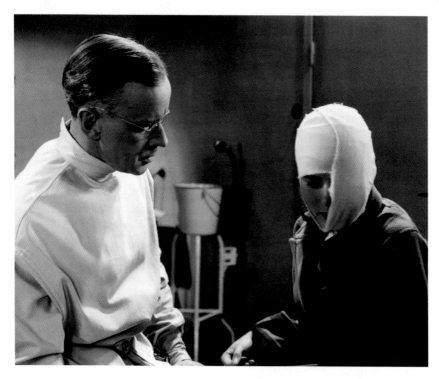

**STILL FROM 'A WOMAN'S FACE'
('EN KVINNAS ANSIKTE', 1938)**
Bergman creating a role that would be remade by Joan
Crawford, under George Cukor's direction. / Die von
Bergman interpretierte Rolle wurde in George Cukors
Hollywood-Remake *Erpressung* (aka *Die Frau mit der
Narbe*, 1941) von Joan Crawford gespielt. / Dans un rôle
qui sera plus tard repris par Joan Crawford, sous la
direction de George Cukor.

**STILL FROM 'A WOMAN'S FACE'
('EN KVINNAS ANSIKTE', 1938)**
Even an unflattering hairstyle couldn't ruin Bergman's
face. / Selbst die unvorteilhafte Frisur konnte den Reiz
von Bergmans Gesicht nicht mindern. / Même une
coiffure peu flatteuse ne saurait l'enlaidir.

STILL FROM 'THE FOUR COMPANIONS' ('DIE VIER GESELLEN', 1938)
Bergman made this light comedy as part of a three-film contract with UFA in Germany. / Diese Komödie war Bestandteil eines Vertrags mit der UFA über drei Filme. / Cette comédie légère est l'un des trois films inscrits dans le contrat signé avec les studios UFA en Allemagne.

PAGES 46/47
STILL FROM 'ONLY ONE NIGHT' ('EN ENDA NATT', 1939)
A high-fashion look that seems subtly wrong for Bergman's primarily democratic personality. / Die Haute-Couture-Kleidung will nicht recht zu Bergmans eher volksnaher Persönlichkeit passen. / Un look sophistiqué qui jure quelque peu avec la simplicité de l'actrice.

**STILL FROM 'THE FOUR COMPANIONS'
('DIE VIER GESELLEN', 1938)**
During the making of the film, Bergman saw how
people's lives were being destroyed by the fascistic
Nazi regime. / Während der Dreharbeiten erlebte
Bergman, wie das Nazi-Regime das Leben der
Menschen zerstörte. / Pendant le tournage, elle
prend pleinement conscience de l'impitoyable
machine à broyer des vies qu'est le régime nazi.

PAGES 48–51
**COVER & PAGES FROM 'CLOSE-UP:
INTERMEZZO' (1939)**
To introduce Bergman to America, David O. Selznick's
publicity campaign emphasized the actress's youthful
freshness. / Um Bergman in Amerika bekannt zu
machen, hob David O. Selznick in seinem Werbefeldzug
die jugendliche Frische der Schauspielerin hervor. /
Pour lancer Ingrid Bergman aux États-Unis, la campagne
publicitaire de David O. Selznick mise sur sa fraîcheur
juvénile.

PAGES 52/53
**STILL FROM 'INTERMEZZO: A LOVE STORY'
(1939)**
With Leslie Howard. / Mit Leslie Howard. / Aux côtés de
Leslie Howard.

CLOSE-UP
of
*Intermezzo

*BERGMAN'S BEST

THE
SELZNICK
STUDIO

IN A TRADITION OF QUALITY

S.I.P.—109-118
AT PEAK of their stolen happiness, Anita (Ingrid Bergman) and Holger (Leslie Howard) indulge in lovers' joke on village quay.

INTERMEZZO: ITS STORY

FOR TWO SINCERE ARTISTS, PLAYED BY BERGMAN AND HOWARD,
A BLISSFUL INTERLUDE BRINGS LOVE, MUSIC AND DEEP HURT

THE overt happiness of the intent young couple pictured above reflects 2 themes of "Intermezzo." The first is the simple and poignant story of a beautiful young pianist, Anita, who falls in love with Holger, father of the little girl who is her star pupil. Her attraction is heightened because the man is a concert violinist whose talents strongly appeal to her zest for music, especially when he plays his composition, "Intermezzo." Secondly, the picture tells the tragedy of the man's broken home and the consequent battles of conscience that haunt the lovers even in their most joyful moments.

Around these basic plots the picture delineates credible and sympathetic sub-themes. The wife reacts with complete honesty when she sees the situation developing and realizes how powerless she is to prevent it. Equally sincere is the role of the little girl, whose faith in and affection for her erring father remain unswerved. A most moving force is the pianist's ambition to win a music scholarship, which she at first hopes will bring her fame in her own right

and which she is later tempted to abandon in favor of her new-found love.

Once the love fires have been kindled, Anita (Ingrid Bergman) becomes concert accompanist for Holger (Leslie Howard) and they embark on a triumphal world tour. For months they share the communal joy of creating superb music together and of discovering each other anew amidst the glamour of the fine arts centers of the world. After a final spectacular concert success in Rio de Janeiro, they take an Elysian holiday in a south-of-France fishing village. They relax, ecstatically at first, then determinedly. Anita even declines a chance to further her own career. But thoughts of the past persist in intruding. Eventually the very tranquility of the Mediterranean village makes them sense the lonely grief of the man's deserted family (Edna Best, Ann Todd, Douglas Scott). The guilt sense will not be downed and eventually Anita faces the problem: Now that she has gone so far, how to end her "Intermezzo?"

9

1. BEFORE ANITA entered Holger's life, he is greeted tenderly by his wife and two children at completion of a long concert tour.

2. HOLGER, pleased to learn from his wife Margit (Edna that new teacher has helped improve their daughter's piano

5. SUDDENLY IN LOVE, Anita finds meeting furtively in cafes is intolerable. To be with her openly, Holger leaves home.

6. SHARING IN LOVE and music, they tour as concert Everywhere their inspired performances meet sensational recep

9. FORMER TEACHER (John Halliday) informs Anita she has been awarded music scholarship and tells of grief in Holger's home.

10. SITUATION'S UNTENABILITY GROWS. Holger nostalgia and Anita reveals she is foregoing privilege of schola

P.—109-16

IN HOLGER'S VIEW Anita's skill in coaching his daughter, An-Marie (Ann Todd), at first transcends her personal appeal.

S.I.P.—109-37

4. AT FAMILY PARTY, where Ann-Marie's progress is appraised by guests, Holger is suddenly impressed by Anita's beauty.

P.—109-145

TOUR CONCLUDED, Anita vacations with Holger on the Mediterranean shore. This is peak of their adventure in happiness.

S.I.P.—109-137

8. FIRST THOUGHTS of past come when village child, who closely resembles Ann-Marie, teaches Holger to play the zither.

P.—109-129

ANITA BEGS OFF planned picnic with Holger. Her absence is prelude to heartbreak. She is gone when Holger returns.

S.I.P.—109-81

12. MONTHS LATER Ann-Marie is struck by car. As doctor describes injuries Holger determines to seek family's forgiveness.

11

**STILL FROM 'A NIGHT IN JUNE'
('JUNINATTEN', 1940)**
A straggler from the Swedish period catches the star in
mid-transformation. / Ein schwedischer Nachzügler holt
den sich in Wandlung begriffenen Star ein. / Un film
tardif de la période suédoise saisit l'actrice en pleine
mutation.

'There is that incandescence about Miss Bergman,
that spiritual spark which makes us believe that
Selznick has found another great lady of the
screen.'
Frank S. Nugent, critic of the 'New York Times', on
'Intermezzo' (1939)

„Von Fräulein Bergman geht ein Strahlen aus,
ein geistiger Funke, der uns vermuten lässt, dass
Selznick eine weitere große Dame der Leinwand
gefunden hat."
Frank S. Nugent, Filmkritiker der *New York Times*, über
Intermezzo (1939)

**STILL FROM 'A NIGHT IN JUNE'
('JUNINATTEN', 1940)**

PAGE 56
PORTRAIT FOR 'ARCH OF TRIUMPH' (1948)
Bergman as the good-bad girl Joan Madou. / Bergman
als das gute „leichte" Mädchen Joan Madou. / En brave
fille de mauvaise vie.

*« Il y a chez Mademoiselle Bergman quelque chose
d'incandescent, une étincelle de spiritualité qui
nous porte à croire que Selznick a découvert une
nouvelle grande dame du cinéma. »*
Frank S. Nugent, critique du *New York Times*, à propos
d'*Intermezzo* (1939)

HOLLYWOOD

HOLLYWOOD

HOLLYWOOD

STILL FROM 'ADAM HAD FOUR SONS' (1941)
Bergman's youth and vivacity make co-star Warner
Baxter look elderly. / Neben Bergmans jugendlicher
Lebhaftigkeit wirkt ihr Schauspielerkollege Warner
Baxter wie ein alter Mann. / Sa jeunesse et sa vivacité
donnent un coup de vieux à son partenaire Warner
Baxter.

STILL FROM 'ADAM HAD FOUR SONS' (1941)
Devotedly tending Fay Wray. / Liebevoll kümmert sie
sich um Molly (Fay Wray). / Dévouée au chevet de Fay
Wray.

"She was a real pro. I feel at home with real pros the way Hemingway liked bullfighters. They're very tough and have a kind of glamour."
Christopher Isherwood

„Sie war ein echter Profi. Ich fühle mich mit echten Profis wohl, so wie Hemingway die Stierkämpfer mochte. Sie sind hart und besitzen eine Art Glamour."
Christopher Isherwood

« C'était une vraie pro. J'apprécie les vrais pros de la même manière que Hemingway aimait les toreros. Ils sont coriaces et ont une sorte de glamour. »
Christopher Isherwood

STILL FROM 'RAGE IN HEAVEN' (1941)
Robert Montgomery encores the maniacal persona he introduced in 'Night Must Fall.' / Robert Montgomery spielt – wie schon in *Night Must Fall* (1937) – einen Wahnsinnigen. / Robert Montgomery dans un personnage désaxé qui rappelle *La Force des ténèbres*.

**STILL FROM 'DR. JEKYLL AND MR. HYDE'
(1941)**
Two frames from the heavily sexualized Freudian dream
sequences of Victor Fleming's film. / Zwei Bilder aus der
stark sexuell geprägten freudianischen Traumsequenz
in Victor Flemings Verfilmung. / Extraits des séquences
oniriques d'un érotisme freudien tournées par Victor
Fleming.

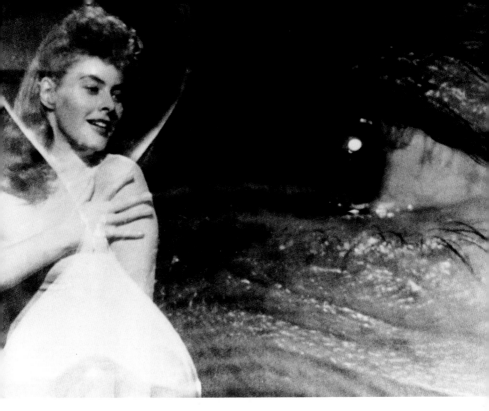

STILL FROM 'DR. JEKYLL AND MR. HYDE'
(1941)

STILL FROM 'CASABLANCA' (1942)
Bergman with Paul Henreid as Victor Laszlo. / Bergman
mit Paul Henreid als Victor Laszlo. / Avec Paul Henreid
dans le rôle de Victor Laszlo.

"Here's looking at you, kid."
Rick Blaine, 'Casablanca' (1942)

„Ich seh dir in die Augen, Kleines."
Rick Blaine, *Casablanca* (1942)

« À tes beaux yeux. »
Rick Blaine, *Casablanca* (1942)

STILL FROM 'CASABLANCA' (1942)
Bergman with Humphrey Bogart and Dooley Wilson in
the Paris flashback. / Bergman mit Humphrey Bogart
und Dooley Wilson in der Rückblende auf die Pariser
Zeit. / Avec Humphrey Bogart et Dooley Wilson dans
le flash-back parisien.

"Play it, Sam. Play 'As Time Goes By.' "
Ilsa Lund, 'Casablanca' (1942)

„Spiel es, Sam. Spiel As Time Goes By."
Ilsa Lund, *Casablanca* (1942)

« Joue, Sam. Joue As Time Goes By. »
Ilsa Lund, *Casablanca* (1942)

PAGES 66/67
STILL FROM 'CASABLANCA' (1942)
Bogart's despair, Bergman's desperation. / Rick
(Bogart) und Ilsa (Bergman) sind – jeder auf seine
Art – verzweifelt. / Le désespoir de Bogart, la
désespérance de Bergman.

STILL FROM 'CASABLANCA' (1942)
The final goodbye. / Das endgültige Lebewohl. / L'ultime
adieu.

*"Anytime that Ingrid Bergman looks at a man, he
has sex appeal."*
Humphrey Bogart

*„Jedes Mal, wenn Ingrid Bergman einen Mann
anschaut, dann hat er Sex-Appeal."*
Humphrey Bogart

*« Chaque fois qu'Ingrid Bergman regarde un
homme, il a du sex-appeal. »*
Humphrey Bogart

ON THE SET OF 'CASABLANCA' (1942)
Preparing the final goodbye with cameraman Arthur
Edeson. / Mit Kameramann Arthur Edeson bei den
Vorbereitungen zu der großen Abschiedsszene. /
Préparation de l'adieu final avec le chef opérateur
Arthur Edeson.

STILL FROM 'FOR WHOM THE BELL TOLLS' (1943)
The splendid mountain scenery that provides a suitably operatic background for the story's passions. / Die herrliche Berglandschaft bietet den zu der leiden-schaftlichen Geschichte passenden opernhaften Hintergrund. / Paysage de montagnes offrant un cadre grandiose aux passions qui s'y déchaînent.

"In my whole life, I never had a woman so much in love with me as Ingrid was. The day after the picture ended, I couldn't get her on the phone."
Gary Cooper

„In meinem ganzen Leben hatte ich nie eine Frau, die so in mich verliebt war wie Ingrid. Am Tag nachdem der Film abgedreht war, bekam ich sie nicht mal mehr ans Telefon."
Gary Cooper

ON THE SET OF 'FOR WHOM THE BELL TOLLS' (1943)
Rehearsing a scene with Gary Cooper. / Beim Proben einer Szene mit Gary Cooper. / Répétition d'une scène avec Gary Cooper.

« De ma vie, je n'ai jamais vu une femme aussi amoureuse de moi. Mais dès la fin du tournage, elle est devenue injoignable. »
Gary Cooper

**ON THE SET OF 'FOR WHOM THE BELL
TOLLS' (1943)**
Rehearsing with director Sam Wood (holding script). /
Beim Proben mit Regisseur Sam Wood (mit dem
Drehbuch in der Hand). / Répétition avec le metteur
en scène Sam Wood (le scénario à la main).

**ON THE SET OF 'FOR WHOM THE BELL
TOLLS' (1943)**
Fishing on a rare day off on location. / Beim Angeln an
einem der seltenen freien Tage während des Außen-
drehs. / Partie de pêche lors d'une des rares journées
de repos.

STILL FROM 'GASLIGHT' (1944)
Charles Boyer and Angela Lansbury flirt while Bergman
wonders if something is afoot. / Gregory (Charles
Boyer) und Nancy (Angela Lansbury) flirten, während
sich Paula (Bergman) fragt, was wohl hinter ihrem
Rücken vorgeht. / Charles Boyer flirte avec Angela
Lansbury tandis qu'Ingrid Bergman se demande ce qui
se trame dans son dos.

PORTRAIT FOR 'GASLIGHT' (1944)
Knowledge dawns. / Allmählich dämmert es. / La vérité
se fait jour.

ON THE SET OF 'GASLIGHT' (1944)
On the set, with director George Cukor (left) and
cameraman Joseph Ruttenberg (second from right). /
Am Set mit Regisseur George Cukor (links) und Kameramann Joseph Ruttenberg (Zweiter von rechts). / Sur le
plateau avec le réalisateur George Cukor (à gauche) et
le chef opérateur Joseph Ruttenberg (deuxième à
droite).

STILL FROM 'GASLIGHT' (1944)
The confrontation scene with Charles Boyer that
helped win her an Academy Award. / Unter anderem
war es die Konfrontation mit Gregory (Charles Boyer),
die ihr einen Oscar einbrachte. / La scène de confrontation avec Charles Boyer qui l'aidera à remporter un
oscar.

STILL FROM 'SARATOGA TRUNK' (1945)
Sporting a desperately unflattering black wig,
accompanied by Flora Robson as an octaroon. / Sie
erscheint mit einer sehr unvorteilhaften schwarzen
Perücke an der Seite von Flora Robson, die eine
„Achtelschwarze" spielt. / Affublée d'une perruque
noire désespérément peu seyante, aux côtés de
Flora Robson dans le rôle d'une mulâtresse.

STILL FROM 'SARATOGA TRUNK' (1945)
Gary Cooper's masculine beauty reduces Bergman to
the status of an adoring female. / Gary Coopers Männ-
lichkeit drängte Bergman in die Rolle der anhimmelnden
Frau. / La beauté virile de Gary Cooper relègue Ingrid
Bergman au rang d'adoratrice.

**STILL FROM 'THE BELLS OF ST. MARY'S'
(1945)**
With Bing Crosby as Father O'Malley in the popular
sequel to 'Going My Way.' / Mit Bing Crosby als Pfarrer
O'Malley in der beliebten Fortsetzung von *Der Weg
zum Glück* (1944). / Avec Bing Crosby dans le rôle du
père O'Malley dans la suite à succès de *La Route semée
d'étoiles.*

**PORTRAIT FOR 'THE BELLS OF ST. MARY'S'
(1945)**
Bergman at her most overtly spiritual. / Bergman zeigt
sich in dieser Rolle spirituell wie nie zuvor. / Dans un de
ses rôles les plus spirituels.

**ON THE SET OF 'THE BELLS OF ST. MARY'S'
(1945)**
Director Leo McCarey playing the piano, his preferred
method of relaxing on the set. / Regisseur Leo McCarey
entspannte während der Dreharbeiten gern am Klavier. /
Le metteur en scène Leo McCarey joue du piano pour
se détendre pendant le tournage.

ACADEMY AWARDS (1944)
Some of the winners of the 1944 acting Oscars: Bing
Crosby, Barry Fitzgerald, and Bergman. / Drei Oscar-
Gewinner des Vorjahres in den Schauspielkategorien:
Bing Crosby, Barry Fitzgerald und Bergman. / Trois
lauréats des Oscars de 1944 : Bing Crosby, Barry
Fitzgerald et Ingrid Bergman.

"Ingrid, it's only a movie."
Alfred Hitchcock

„Ingrid, es ist bloß ein Film!"
Alfred Hitchcock

« Ce n'est que du cinéma, Ingrid. »
Alfred Hitchcock

PORTRAIT FOR 'SPELLBOUND' (1945)

ON THE SET OF 'SPELLBOUND' (1945)
Rehearsing with Gregory Peck and Alfred Hitchcock. /
Bei den Proben mit Gregory Peck und Alfred Hitchcock. /
Répétition avec Gregory Peck et Alfred Hitchcock.

STILL FROM 'SPELLBOUND' (1945)
Attempting to calm a distraught Gregory Peck. / Beim
Versuch, den verzweifelten John/Anthony (Gregory
Peck) zu beruhigen. / Ingrid Bergman tente de calmer
un Gregory Peck éperdu.

STILL FROM 'SPELLBOUND' (1945)
An exceedingly rare shot from a cut dream scene. /
Ein ausgesprochen rares Bild aus einer heraus-
geschnittenen Traumszene. / Image extrêmement
rare d'un scène onirique coupée au montage.

ON THE SET OF 'SPELLBOUND' (1945)
Resting on a slant board while shooting one of Salvador
Dalí's dream sequences. / Bei den Dreharbeiten zu den
von Salvador Dalí konzipierten Traumsequenzen lehnt
sie sich an ein schräges Brett. / Appuyée contre une
planche pendant le tournage d'une des séquences
oniriques de Salvador Dalí.

STILL FROM 'NOTORIOUS' (1946)
Hitchcock devised a series of brief, nuzzling kisses to get around the Breen office restrictions. / Hitchcock erdachte eine Abfolge kurzer Küsse, um die Einschränkungen der freiwilligen Selbstzensur zu umgehen. / Afin de contourner la censure, Hitchcock opte pour une série de petits baisers fureteurs.

ON THE SET OF 'NOTORIOUS' (1946)
Rehearsing a complicated boom shot with cameraman Ted Tetzlaff. / Bei den Proben zur berühmten Kamerakranfahrt mit Kameramann Ted Tetzlaff. / Répétition d'un plan en plongée avec le chef opérateur Ted Tetzlaff.

STILL FROM 'NOTORIOUS' (1946)
In the cellar, looking for uranium in wine bottles. /
Im Keller suchen die beiden in den Weinflaschen
nach Uran. / À la recherche de l'uranium caché dans
des bouteilles de vin à la cave.

STILL FROM 'NOTORIOUS' (1946)
A helpless victim of her ultimately helpless husband's
plotting. / Als hilfloses Opfer der Machenschaften ihres
letztlich ebenso hilflosen Ehemanns. / Impuissante
victime des machinations de son mari, qui s'avère tout
aussi impuissant.

"I'm only interested in two kinds of people, those who can entertain me and those who can advance my career."
Ingrid Bergman

„Ich bin nur an zwei Arten von Menschen interessiert: solchen, die mich unterhalten, und solchen, die meine Karriere voranbringen."
Ingrid Bergman

« Je ne m'intéresse qu'à deux catégories de gens : ceux qui peuvent me distraire et ceux qui peuvent m'aider dans ma carrière. »
Ingrid Bergman

STILL FROM 'ARCH OF TRIUMPH' (1948)
As the streetwalker Joan Madou. / Als Strichmädchen Joan Madou. / Dans le rôle de la prostituée Joan Madou.

"Ingrid had that beautiful side and the other side, too. She was a smart woman and had a coldness about her. She could fend for herself and still need a man. One side was completely open, and the other completely steel."
Alf Kjellin

„Ingrid besaß diese schöne Seite und auch diese andere Seite. Sie war eine kluge Frau und strahlte eine gewisse Kälte aus. Sie konnte ihre Frau stehen und brauchte dennoch einen Mann. Eine Seite war völlig offen, die andere ganz und gar aus Stahl.“
Alf Kjellin

« Ingrid avait un très bon côté, mais elle avait une autre facette. C'était une femme intelligente qui avait quelque chose de froid. Elle pouvait se débrouiller toute seule et avoir quand même besoin d'un homme. D'un côté elle était totalement ouverte, de l'autre elle était de marbre. »
Alf Kjellin

STILL FROM 'JOAN OF ARC' (1948)
The Maid of Orleans goes into battle. / Die Jungfrau von Orléans zieht in die Schlacht. / La pucelle d'Orléans part au combat.

STILL FROM 'JOAN OF ARC' (1948)
The final battle. / Die letzte Schlacht. / L'ultime bataille.

STILL FROM 'JOAN OF ARC' (1948)
The aftermath of battle – an oddly stilted shot from
an oddly stilted film. / Nach der Schlacht: eine seltsam
steife Aufnahme aus einem seltsam steifen Film. /
Après la bataille, scène symptomatique d'un film
curieusement guindé.

STILL FROM 'JOAN OF ARC' (1948)
The preparation for the trial. / Vorbereitung auf den
Prozess. / Dans l'attente du procès.

STILL FROM 'JOAN OF ARC' (1948)
The lady's for burning. / Bereit für den Scheiterhaufen. /
Condamnée au bûcher.

STILL FROM 'UNDER CAPRICORN' (1949)
With Joseph Cotton. / Mit Joseph Cotton. / Aux côtés
de Joseph Cotton.

PAGES 104/105
ON THE SET OF 'UNDER CAPRICORN' (1949)
With Michael Wilding and the blimped Technicolor
camera. / Mit Michael Wilding und der Technicolor-
Kamera in schalldichtem Gehäuse. / Avec Michael
Wilding et la caméra Technicolor insonorisée.

STILL FROM 'UNDER CAPRICORN' (1949)
An unusually literal piece of Grand Guignol from
Hitchcock. / Triviale Schockelemente wie diese waren
für Hitchcock eher ungewöhnlich. / Scène de Grand-
Guignol étonnamment littérale pour du Hitchcock.

EXILE

EXIL

L'EXIL

STILL FROM 'STROMBOLI' (1950)
Neo-realism collides with a great star on her way to
being a great actress. / Hier kollidieren Neorealismus
und ein großer Star auf dem Weg, eine große Schauspielerin zu werden. / Une grande star en passe
de devenir une grande actrice en plein âge d'or du
néoréalisme.

PAGE 106
ON THE SET OF 'STROMBOLI' (1950)
With Roberto Rossellini on location at Stromboli. /
Mit Roberto Rossellini bei den Dreharbeiten am
Stromboli. / Avec Roberto Rossellini lors du tournage
à Stromboli.

STILL FROM 'STROMBOLI' (1950)
As close as Rossellini could get to glamorizing
his leading lady. / Näher konnte Rossellini der
Verherrlichung seiner Hauptdarstellerin nicht
kommen. / L'image la plus glamour que Rossellini
s'autorise à donner de sa belle.

ON THE SET OF 'STROMBOLI' (1950)
Shooting a jury-rigged tracking shot. / Eine improvisierte
Fahraufnahme. / Travelling tourné à l'aide d'une
installation de fortune.

PAGES 112/113
ON THE SET OF 'STROMBOLI' (1950)
A break from the rigors of location work. / Eine Pause
beim anstrengenden Außendreh. / Pause loin des
rigueurs du tournage en extérieur.

ON THE SET OF 'STROMBOLI' (1950)
Wearing masks to avoid deadly fumes from the
volcano. / Zum Schutz vor den giftigen Vulkandämpfen
tragen alle Beteiligten Atemmasken. / Port du masque
de rigueur pour se protéger des vapeurs toxiques du
volcan.

**STILL FROM 'THE GREATEST LOVE'
('EUROPA '51', 1951)**
A touch of maturity visible for the first time. /
Erstmals zeigt sich ein Anflug von Reife. / Une
touche de maturité visible pour la première fois.

"He made his film as a writer takes up a pen – he
made his film with his camera. He invented from
day to day the dialogue. He knew exactly what he
wanted, but he didn't know exactly the words and
very often he would say, 'Well this is a scene here.
You walk down the street and you meet so and so.
So you say to her anything you want.' And I used
to say, 'But I don't know what.' 'Well, you know,
invent something.' "
Ingrid Bergman on Roberto Rossellini

„Er drehte einen Film so, wie ein Schriftsteller zur
Feder greift – er machte seine Filme mit der
Kamera. Die Dialoge dachte er sich einfach von
einem Tag auf den anderen aus. Er wusste genau,
was er wollte, aber er konnte es nicht genau in
Worte fassen, und so sagte er oft: ‚Nun, die Szene
sieht so aus: Du spazierst die Straße lang und
begegnest Soundso. Rede mit ihr einfach, was du
willst.' Und ich pflegte zu sagen: ‚Aber ich weiß
nicht, was.' ‚Dir fällt schon was ein.'"
Ingrid Bergman über Roberto Rossellini

**STILL FROM 'THE GREATEST LOVE'
('EUROPA '51', 1951)**
A subtle film about disaffection and ennui that
presages Antonioni. / Ein hintergründiger Film über
Unzufriedenheit und Langeweile in Vorwegnahme
von Antonioni. / Un film subtil sur la désaffection et
l'ennui qui préfigure Antonioni.

*« Il faisait un film comme un écrivain prend son
stylo, il écrivait avec sa caméra. Il inventait les
dialogues au jour le jour. Il savait exactement ce
qu'il voulait, mais il ne savait pas comment le
formuler et il me disait souvent : "Voilà la scène. Tu
marches dans la rue et tu rencontres telle ou telle
personne. Dis-lui ce que tu veux." Je répondais :
"Mais je ne sais pas quoi lui dire." "Eh bien, tu n'as
qu'à inventer." »*
Ingrid Bergman à propos de Roberto Rossellini

"Rossellini has never been a man that can entertain. It isn't at all that he wants to give people fun. He wants to teach them."
Ingrid Bergman on Roberto Rossellini

„*Rossellini war nie ein Mensch, der unterhalten konnte. Er hat überhaupt nicht die Absicht, anderen Vergnügen zu bereiten. Er möchte ihnen etwas beibringen.*"
Ingrid Bergman über Roberto Rossellini

« *Rossellini a toujours été incapable de distraire. Il n'a pas du tout l'intention d'amuser les gens. Il veut les éduquer.* »
Ingrid Bergman à propos de Roberto Rossellini

**STILL FROM 'THE GREATEST LOVE'
('EUROPA '51', 1951)**
The suicide of their son brings a husband and wife together. / Ein Mann und seine Frau kommen sich durch den Suizid ihres Sohnes näher. / Le suicide de leur fils rapproche les deux époux.

STILL FROM 'JOURNEY TO ITALY' ('VIAGGIO IN ITALIA', 1954)
Bergman and George Sanders play a couple attempting to reconcile their differences. / Bergman und George Sanders spielen ein Ehepaar, das seine Differenzen beizulegen versucht. / Ingrid Bergman et George Sanders incarnent un couple tentant de concilier ses différences.

"Probably, subconsciously, he offered a way out from both my problems: my marriage and my life in Hollywood. But it wasn't clear to me at that time."
Ingrid Bergman on Roberto Rossellini

„Wahrscheinlich bot er mir unbewusst einen Ausweg aus meinen beiden Problemen: meiner Ehe und meinem Leben in Hollywood. Aber das war mir zu diesem Zeitpunkt nicht klar."
Ingrid Bergman über Roberto Rossellini

« Il m'offrait sans doute, inconsciemment, le moyen d'échapper à mon mariage et à ma vie à Hollywood. Mais je ne m'en rendais pas compte à l'époque. »
Ingrid Bergman à propos de Roberto Rossellini

STILL FROM 'JOURNEY TO ITALY' ('VIAGGIO IN ITALIA', 1954)
This was the inspiration for a number of subsequent films. / Dieser Film inspirierte eine Reihe ähnlicher Filmwerke. / Un film qui en inspirera plusieurs autres.

STILL FROM 'FEAR' ('LA PAURA', 'ANGST', 1955)
The last of the Rossellini-Bergman films, but by no means the least. / Der letzte der Rossellini-Bergman-Filme war keineswegs der schlechteste. / Le dernier film tourné avec Rossellini, mais non le moindre.

PORTRAIT
Bergman's mature command made this one of the most aesthetically fulfilling periods of her life. / Dank ihrer reifen Meisterschaft fand Bergman zu einer ästhetischen Erfüllung wie in kaum einer anderen Schaffensperiode ihres Lebens. / Grâce à sa maîtrise et à sa maturité, c'est l'une des plus belles périodes de sa vie.

RETURN

RÜCKKEHR

LE RETOUR

ON THE SET OF 'ANASTASIA' (1956)
A heavily dramatic story requires some levity on the
set. / Die äußerst dramatische Geschichte verlangt
bei den Dreharbeiten nach ein wenig auflockernder
Heiterkeit. / Une histoire d'une telle lourdeur dramatique nécessite un peu de légèreté sur le plateau.

PAGE 122
PORTRAIT FOR 'ANASTASIA' (1956)
A glowing Bergman in a formal portrait for her
American comeback picture. / Eine strahlende Bergman
in einem formellen Porträt für den Film, mit dem sie ihr
amerikanisches Comeback feierte. / Ingrid Bergman
resplendissante dans ce portrait annonçant son grand
retour en Amérique.

PAGES 124/125
STILL FROM 'ANASTASIA' (1956)
As Anna Koreff, with Yul Brynner. / Als Anna Koreff, mit
Yul Brynner. / Dans le rôle d'Anna Koreff aux côtés de
Yul Brynner.

ON THE SET OF 'ANASTASIA' (1956)
On the set in Paris with Yul Brynner, a beggar and his cat. / Bei den Dreharbeiten in Paris mit Yul Brynner, einem Bettler und seiner Katze. / Sur le tournage à Paris avec Yul Brynner, un clochard et son chat.

"I think that Ingrid was at home only in one place in the world: working."
Helen Hayes

„Ich glaube, Ingrid fühlte sich nur an einem einzigen Ort in der Welt zu Hause: bei der Arbeit."
Helen Hayes

« Je crois que le seul endroit où Ingrid se sentait chez elle, c'était au travail. »
Helen Hayes

STILL FROM 'ANASTASIA' (1956)
The White Russian conspiracy begins to take hold. /
Die weißrussische Verschwörung fasst allmählich Fuß. /
La supercherie des Russes blancs commence à prendre.

STILL FROM 'ANASTASIA' (1956)
The crucial climactic confrontation, with Helen Hayes as
the Grand Duchess. / Die entscheidende Konfrontation
bildet den Höhepunkt des Films. Mit Helen Hayes als
Großherzogin. / La scène clé de la confrontation finale,
avec Helen Hayes dans le rôle de la grande-duchesse.

PORTRAIT FOR 'PARIS DOES STRANGE THINGS' ('ELENA ET LES HOMMES', 1956)
The essence of Ingrid Bergman. / Das Wesen der Ingrid Bergman auf den Punkt gebracht. / L'essence même d'Ingrid Bergman.

ON THE SET OF 'PARIS DOES STRANGE THINGS' ('ELENA ET LES HOMMES', 1956)
Having her dress buttoned by the beloved director Jean Renoir. / Der von ihr geliebte Regisseur Jean Renoir darf das Kleid zuknöpfen. / L'actrice fait boutonner sa robe par un metteur en scène cher à son cœur, Jean Renoir.

**STILL FROM 'PARIS DOES STRANGE THINGS'
('ELENA ET LES HOMMES', 1956)**
With Jean Marais. / Mit Jean Marais. / Aux côtés de
Jean Marais.

**PORTRAIT FOR 'PARIS DOES STRANGE
THINGS' ('ELENA ET LES HOMMES', 1956)**
Bergman's beauty even lightens the normally sepulchral
Mel Ferrer. / Bergmans Schönheit bringt sogar den
ansonsten düster dreinblickenden Mel Ferrer zum
Strahlen. / Sa beauté déride même Mel Ferrer,
d'ordinaire si austère.

STILL FROM 'INDISCREET' (1958)
A moving tribute to the power of love in middle age. /
Eine bewegende Hommage an die Macht der Liebe in
mittleren Jahren. / Émouvant hommage à la puissance
de l'amour entre personnes d'âge mûr.

STILL FROM 'INDISCREET' (1958)

"She was so good on camera because she had a completely rooted quality. She was completely at ease. She never seized up while acting. Her concentration was complete. She was in her element."
Stanley Donen, director

„Sie war vor der Kamera so gut, weil sie ganz und gar in ihrem Metier war. Sie war völlig entspannt. Beim Schauspielen war sie niemals verkrampft. Sie war völlig konzentriert. Sie war in ihrem Element."
Stanley Donen, Regisseur

« Si elle était si formidable à l'écran, c'est parce qu'elle possédait une qualité profondément ancrée. Elle était parfaitement à l'aise. Elle n'avait jamais de blocage. Sa concentration était totale. Elle était dans son élément. »
Stanley Donen, réalisateur

"Lunching with her is like sitting down to an hour or so of conversation with a charming and highly intelligent orchid."
Thornton Delahanty

„Mit ihr zu essen, ist wie eine einstündige Unterhaltung mit einer reizenden und hochintelligenten Orchidee."
Thornton Delahanty

« Déjeuner avec elle, c'est comme passer une heure à converser avec une charmante et très intelligente orchidée. »
Thornton Delahanty

STILL FROM 'INDISCREET' (1958)
For a romantic comedy, Stanley Donen's film is unusually intense and emotional. / Für eine Liebeskomödie ist Stanley Donens Film ungewöhnlich intensiv und gefühlvoll. / Pour une comédie romantique, ce film de Stanley Donen est étonnamment intense et émouvant.

STILL FROM 'INDISCREET' (1958)
Grant and Bergman could be seen as the eroticized
Tracy and Hepburn. / Grant und Bergman zeigen sich
als erotisierte Version von Tracy und Hepburn. / Grant
et Bergman, un couple à la Tracy et Hepburn, en plus
érotique.

PORTRAIT FOR 'INDISCREET' (1958)

**STILL FROM 'THE INN OF THE SIXTH
HAPPINESS' (1958)**
With Robert Donat (in his last film) and Curd Jurgens. /
Mit Robert Donat (in seinem letzten Film) und Curd
Jürgens. / Avec Robert Donat (dans son dernier film)
et Curd Jurgens.

**STILL FROM 'THE INN OF THE SIXTH
HAPPINESS' (1958)**
Mark Robson's film returned Bergman to intense
drama. / Mit Mark Robsons Film kehrte Bergman zum
großen Drama zurück. / Avec ce film de Mark Robson,
elle retrouve un rôle intensément dramatique.

STILL FROM 'THE INN OF THE SIXTH HAPPINESS' (1958)

STILL FROM 'THE INN OF THE SIXTH HAPPINESS' (1958)
A doomed love between an Englishwoman and a Chinese general. / Die Liebe zwischen der Engländerin und dem chinesischen General ist zum Scheitern verurteilt. / Un amour condamné entre une Anglaise et un général chinois.

ON THE SET OF 'THE INN OF THE SIXTH HAPPINESS' (1958)

On the set with her three children by Rossellini. / Am Set mit ihren drei Kindern aus der Beziehung zu Rossellini. / Sur le tournage, avec les trois enfants nés de son union avec Rossellini.

PAGES 146/147
STILL FROM 'GOODBYE AGAIN' ('AIMEZ-VOUS BRAHMS ?', 1961)

With Yves Montand as a former – and still desired – lover. / Mit Yves Montand als ehemaligem Geliebten, den sie noch immer begehrt. / Avec Yves Montand en ancien amant toujours désiré.

STILL FROM 'THE INN OF THE SIXTH HAPPINESS' (1958)

Leading her charges to freedom. / Sie führt die ihr anvertrauten Kinder in die Freiheit. / Conduisant ses protégés sur le chemin de la liberté.

STILL FROM 'GOODBYE AGAIN' ('AIMEZ-VOUS BRAHMS ?', 1961)
With Anthony Perkins, playing her younger lover. /
Mit Anthony Perkins, der ihren jungen Liebhaber
spielt. / Avec Anthony Perkins, son jeune amant.

"The two greatest talents I worked with were Ingrid
Bergman and Anna Magnani. But I would prefer to
work with Anna, whom I didn't like, than with
Ingrid, whom I loved."
Anthony Quinn

„Die beiden größten Talente, mit denen ich
zusammengearbeitet habe, waren Ingrid Bergman
und Anna Magnani. Aber ich würde lieber wieder
mit Anna arbeiten, die ich nicht mochte, als mit
Ingrid, die ich liebte."
Anthony Quinn

« Les deux plus grands talents avec lesquels j'ai
travaillé sont Ingrid Bergman et Anna Magnani.
Mais j'aimais mieux travailler avec Anna, que je
n'aimais pas, qu'avec Ingrid, que j'adorais. »
Anthony Quinn

STILL FROM 'GOODBYE AGAIN' ('AIMEZ-VOUS BRAHMS ?', 1961)
With Anthony Perkins. / Mit Anthony Perkins. / Aux côtés d'Anthony Perkins.

PAGES 150/151
STILL FROM 'THE VISIT' (1964)
A very accurate visual representation of the theme of Friedrich Dürrenmatt's play about female revenge. / Eine treffende visuelle Umsetzung von Friedrich Dürrenmatts Stück über weibliche Rache. / Représentation très fidèle de la pièce de Friedrich Dürrenmatt sur le thème de la vengeance féminine.

STILL FROM 'THE VISIT' (1964)
The wronged girl returns home as an imperious,
controlling woman. / Das Mädchen, dem Unrecht
geschah, kehrt als herrische und autoritäre Frau
zurück. / La jeune fille bafouée est devenue une
femme puissante et impérieuse.

STILL FROM 'THE VISIT' (1964)
The elegant and the earthy colliding and colluding. /
Eleganz und Urwüchsigkeit spielen miteinander und
gegeneinander. / Collusion et collision entre l'élégante
et le rustique.

STILL FROM 'THE YELLOW ROLLS-ROYCE'
(1965)
With Omar Sharif in the Terrence Rattigan/Anthony
Asquith production. / Mit Omar Sharif in der
Produktion von Terrence Rattigan und Anthony
Asquith. / Avec Omar Sharif dans un film d'Anthony
Asquith et Terrence Rattigan.

STILL FROM 'THE YELLOW ROLLS-ROYCE'
(1965)
Beautiful even in a crisis. / Auch in Krisensituationen
schön. / Belle même en plein drame.

STILL FROM 'STIMULANTIA' (1967)
Gustaf Molander, who had discovered Bergman in the
1930s, directed her in his last film. / Bergman, von
Gustaf Molander in den Dreißigerjahren entdeckt,
spielte auch im letzten Film des Regisseurs mit. / Gustaf
Molander, qui l'a découverte dans les années 1930,
la dirige dans son dernier film.

STILL FROM 'STIMULANTIA' (1967)
Unafraid to appeared ravaged. / Sie hatte keine
Angst davor, sich in aufgelöstem Zustand zu zeigen. /
Ne craignant pas de paraître ravagée.

STILL FROM 'CACTUS FLOWER' (1969)
A return to Hollywood and a sure-fire commercial
success. / Rückkehr nach Hollywood und zum sicheren
Kassenerfolg. / Succès commercial garanti pour son
retour à Hollywood.

STILL FROM 'CACTUS FLOWER' (1969)
Competing on the dance floor with Goldie Hawn for
Walter Matthau's attentions. / Auf dem Tanzboden
wetteifert Stephanie (Bergman) mit Toni (Goldie Hawn)
um die Gunst von Dr. Winston (Walter Matthau). / Elle
rivalise avec Goldie Hawn sur la piste de danse pour
gagner les faveurs de Walter Matthau.

PAGES 160/161
**ON THE SET OF 'A WALK IN THE SPRING
RAIN' (1970)**
Relaxing with two of her co-stars. / Hier gönnt sie
sich mit zwei Mitdarstellern eine Pause. / Moment
de détente avec ses deux partenaires.

**STILL FROM 'A WALK IN THE SPRING RAIN'
(1970)**
With Anthony Quinn as an unlikely Tennessee farmer. /
Mit dem unglaubwürdigen Anthony Quinn in der Rolle
eines Bauern aus Tennessee. / Avec Anthony Quinn en
improbable fermier du Tennessee.

"I don't think Ingrid wanted to dominate, but she
was such an enormous personality that she
dominated everyone around her. The only people
that survived working with her were people where
you know there can't be any romance. They could
dominate because they didn't care. Anybody that
cared, she took over."
Anthony Quinn

„Ich glaube nicht, dass Ingrid herrschsüchtig war,
aber sie war eine so enorme Persönlichkeit, dass
sie einfach jedermann in ihrem Umfeld dominierte.
Das Arbeiten mit ihr hielten nur Leute aus, bei
denen man wusste, dass es keine romantische
Beziehung geben konnte. Sie konnten sie
beherrschen, weil sie ihnen egal war. Jeden,
dem sie nicht egal war, kontrollierte sie."
Anthony Quinn

**STILL FROM 'A WALK IN THE SPRING RAIN'
(1970)**
An extramarital affair explodes into violence. / Eine
außereheliche Affäre mündet in Gewalt. / Une liaison
extraconjugale qui débouche sur la violence.

*« Je ne pense pas qu'Ingrid avait la volonté de
dominer, mais elle avait une telle personnalité
qu'elle dominait tout le monde autour d'elle. Les
seuls qui arrivaient à travailler avec elle sans y
laisser des plumes étaient ceux qui n'avaient rien à
espérer d'elle sur le plan sentimental. Ils pouvaient
la dominer parce qu'ils n'étaient pas intéressés.
Dès qu'on était intéressé, elle prenait le dessus. »*
Anthony Quinn

PAGES 164/165
**STILL FROM 'FROM THE MIXED-UP FILES
OF MRS. BASIL E. FRANKWEILER' (1973)**
Bergman begins to focus on character parts,
i.e. women who have ceased to attract men. /
Bergman konzentriert sich zunehmend auf
Charakterrollen – anders gesagt, sie spielt Frauen,
die keine Anziehungskraft mehr auf Männer ausüben. /
Ingrid Bergman commence à se spécialiser dans les
rôles de composition, ceux de femmes qui ont cessé
d'attirer les hommes.

STILL FROM 'MURDER ON THE ORIENT EXPRESS' (1974)
With Albert Finney as Hercule Poirot. / Mit Albert Finney als Hercule Poirot. / Avec Albert Finney dans le rôle de Hercule Poirot.

PORTRAIT FOR 'MURDER ON THE ORIENT EXPRESS' (1974)
As a thoroughly deglamorized drudge. / Als ganz und gar unglamouröse Dienerin. / En bonne à tout faire dénuée de tout charme.

STILL FROM 'A MATTER OF TIME' (1976)
As a dying countess awash in memories of her
youth. / Sie schwelgt als sterbende Gräfin in Jugend-
erinnerungen. / En comtesse moribonde perdue dans
ses souvenirs de jeunesse.

*"I work because I like to work. I'll work until I'm an
old lady and I'll play grandma parts."*
Ingrid Bergman

*„Ich arbeite, weil es mir Spaß macht. Ich arbeite,
bis ich eine alte Dame bin, und dann spiele ich
Omarollen."*
Ingrid Bergman

*« Je travaille parce que j'aime travailler. Quand je
serai vieille, je jouerai des rôles de grand-mère. »*
Ingrid Bergman

STILL FROM 'A MATTER OF TIME' (1976)
Passing the torch of romantic fervor to a chambermaid
played by Liza Minnelli. / Sie reicht die Fackel glühen-
der Leidenschaft weiter an ihre Kammerzofe, gespielt
von Liza Minnelli. / Passant le flambeau de la ferveur
romantique à une femme de chambre interprétée par
Liza Minnelli.

STILL FROM 'AUTUMN SONATA'
('HÖSTSONATEN', 1978)
As the pianist whose art means more to her than her
children. / In der Rolle der Pianistin, der die Kunst mehr
bedeutet als die eigenen Kinder. / En pianiste dont la
carrière artistique importe plus que ses enfants.

"Ingrid was an anarchist, an erratic anarchist."
Ingmar Bergman

*„Ingrid war Anarchistin, eine unberechenbare
Anarchistin."*
Ingmar Bergman

*« Ingrid était une anarchiste, une anarchiste
fantasque. »*
Ingmar Bergman

**STILL FROM 'AUTUMN SONATA'
('HÖSTSONATEN', 1978)**
Summoning all her power for one last acting
masterpiece. / Für eine letzte schauspielerische
Meisterleistung nimmt sie all ihre Kräfte zusammen. /
Elle rassemble ici toutes ses forces pour un ultime
morceau de bravoure.

PAGES 172/173
**ON THE SET OF 'AUTUMN SONATA'
('HÖSTSONATEN', 1978)**
With a cajoling Ingmar Bergman. / Ingmar Bergman
redet Ingrid Bergman gut zu. / Réconfortée par Ingmar
Bergman.

**STILL FROM 'A WOMAN CALLED GOLDA'
(1982)**
As Golda Meir in her last TV film. / In ihrem letzten
Fernsehfilm als Golda Meir. / Dans le rôle de Golda
Meir pour son dernier téléfilm.

"I think my life has been wonderful. I have done
what I felt like. I was given courage and I was given
adventure and that has carried me along. And then
also a sense of humor and a little bit of common
sense. It has been a very rich life."
Ingrid Bergman

„Ich glaube, mein Leben war wundervoll. Ich habe
getan, wozu ich Lust hatte. Mir wurde Mut
geschenkt und Abenteuergeist, und das hat mich
getragen. Und dann auch Sinn für Humor und ein
bisschen gesunder Menschenverstand. Es war ein
sehr reiches Leben."
Ingrid Bergman

« J'ai eu une vie merveilleuse. J'ai fait ce que j'avais
envie de faire. On m'a donné du courage et le goût
de l'aventure et c'est ce qui m'a fait avancer. Peut-
être aussi le sens de l'humour et un peu de bon
sens. J'ai eu une vie très riche. »
Ingrid Bergman

STILL FROM 'A WOMAN CALLED GOLDA' (1982)
Seamlessly blending into an ensemble of character actors. / Nahtlos fügt sie sich in das Ensemble aus Nebendarstellern ein. / Se mêlant discrètement à des acteurs de second plan.

"For Italians, who are so deeply touched by the Catholic Church and the figure of the Virgin Mary, [Bergman] was someone who reminded you of an American saint."
Federico Fellini

„Für die Italiener, denen die katholische Kirche und die Figur der Jungfrau Maria so viel bedeuten, war [Bergman] jemand, der an eine amerikanische Heilige erinnerte."
Federico Fellini

« Pour les Italiens, qui sont tellement attachés à l'Église catholique et à la figure de la Vierge Marie, [Bergman] avait quelque chose d'une sainte américaine. »
Federico Fellini

PORTRAIT FOR 'A WOMAN CALLED GOLDA' (1982)
Dying of cancer, her beauty obscured by age and makeup, the actress still triumphs. / Obschon sie vom Krebs gezeichnet ist und ihre Schönheit von Alter und Maske verdeckt wird, feiert die Schauspielerin noch immer Triumphe. / Rongée par le cancer, les traits alourdis par l'âge et le maquillage, l'actrice surmonte tous les obstacles.

PAGE 178
INGRID BERGMAN (1956)

3

CHRONOLOGY

CHRONOLOGIE

CHRONOLOGIE

29 August 1915 Ingrid Bergman is born in Stockholm to Justus and Friedel Adler Bergman. Her father owns a photography shop.

1918 Ingrid's mother dies of a liver ailment.

1927 Justus Bergman dies of stomach cancer. Ingrid goes to live with her Aunt Ellen, who dies six months later. Ingrid takes part in school plays.

1931 Works at Svensk Filmindustri as an extra.

1933 Accepted at the Royal Dramatic Theater in Stockholm.

1934 Appears in the madcap comedy film *The Count of the Monk's Bridge*; offered a contract by Svensk Filmindustri.

10 July 1937 Marries Dr. Petter Lindstrom.

20 September 1938 Birth of daughter Pia.

1939 Signs a contract with David O. Selznick in February. *Intermezzo: A Love Story*.

1941 *Dr. Jekyll and Mr. Hyde*.

1942 *Casablanca*.

1943 *For Whom the Bell Tolls*. Nominated for an Academy Award.

1944 *Gaslight*. Wins Academy Award for Best Actress.

1945 *The Bells of St. Mary's*. Nominated for an Academy Award. *Spellbound*.

1946 *Notorious*.

1948 *Joan of Arc*. Nominated for an Academy Award.

1949 Works with Roberto Rossellini on *Stromboli* in Italy. June: discovers she is pregnant by him. 5 August: announces the beginning of divorce proceedings from Petter Lindstrom, to be followed by retirement. 6 August: announcement that Bergman is pregnant with Rossellini's child.

1950 2 February: birth of Robertino Rossellini. 19 April: property settlement with Petter Lindstrom, who has custody of Pia Lindstrom. 24 May: marriage in Rome to Roberto Rossellini. 1 November: divorce in America from Petter Lindstrom.

1951 Becomes pregnant with twins.

1954 *Journey to Italy*.

1956 *Anastasia*. Wins Academy Award for Best Actress.

1957 June: Meets Lars Schmidt, Swedish theater producer. November: separation from Roberto Rossellini.

1958 *Indiscreet*. Marriage to Rossellini is annulled because it was illegal. 21 December: marries Lars Schmidt in London. *The Inn of the Sixth Happiness*.

1959 Ruling in French court gives her custody of her three children by Rossellini. Rossellini refuses to make support payments.

1964 *The Visit*.

1974 *Murder on the Orient Express*. Receives Academy Award for Best Supporting Actress.

1978 *Autumn Sonata*. Nominated for an Academy Award.

29 August 1982 Dies of cancer.

**STILL FROM 'THE GREATEST LOVE'
('EUROPA '51', 1951)**

CHRONOLOGIE

29. August 1915 Ingrid Bergman wird in
Stockholm als Tochter von Justus Bergman und
Friedel Adler Bergman geboren. Ihr Vater besitzt
ein Fotogeschäft.

1918 Ingrids Mutter erliegt einem Leberleiden.

1927 Justus Bergman stirbt an Magenkrebs.
Ingrid zieht zu ihrer Tante Ellen, die ein halbes Jahr
später ebenfalls stirbt. In Schulaufführungen steht
Ingrid erstmals auf der Bühne.

1931 Sie arbeitet als Statistin bei Svensk
Filmindustri.

1933 Sie wird in das Kungliga Dramatiska Teatern
in Stockholm aufgenommen.

1934 Sie tritt in der turbulenten Filmkomödie
Munkbrogreven auf. Svensk Filmindustri bietet ihr
daraufhin einen Filmvertrag an.

10. Juli 1937 Sie heiratet Dr. Petter Lindström.

20. September 1938 Ihre Tochter Pia wird
geboren.

1939 Im Februar wird sie von David O. Selznick
unter Vertrag genommen. *Intermezzo: A Love Story*
(*Intermezzo*).

1941 *Dr. Jekyll and Mr. Hyde* (*Arzt und Dämon*).

1942 *Casablanca*.

1943 *For Whom the Bell Tolls* (*Wem die Stunde
schlägt*). Oscar-Nominierung.

1944 *Gaslight* (*Das Haus der Lady Alquist*).
Sie erhält einen Oscar als beste Darstellerin.

1945 *The Bells of St. Mary's* (*Die Glocken von
St. Marien*). Oscar-Nominierung. *Spellbound*
(*Ich kämpfe um dich*).

1946 *Notorious* (*Berüchtigt/Weißes Gift*).

1948 *Joan of Arc* (*Johanna von Orléans*). Oscar-
Nominierung.

1949 Sie arbeitet in Italien mit Roberto Rossellini
an dem Film *Stromboli*. Juni: Sie stellt fest, dass sie

von ihm ein Kind erwartet. 5. August: Sie gibt
bekannt, dass sie die Scheidung von Petter
Lindström eingereicht hat und sich danach aus
dem Filmgeschäft zurückziehen will. 6. August:
Es wird bekanntgegeben, dass Bergman ein Kind
von Rossellini erwartet.

1950 2. Februar: Geburt von Robertino Rossellini.
19. April: Sie trifft eine Güterregelung mit Petter
Lindström, der das Sorgerecht für die gemeinsame
Tochter Pia erhält. 24. Mai: Sie heiratet Roberto
Rossellini in Rom. 1. November: Sie wird in Amerika
von Petter Lindström geschieden.

1951 Sie wird erneut schwanger, diesmal mit
Zwillingen.

1954 *Viaggio in Italia* (*Reise in Italien/Liebe ist
stärker*).

1956 *Anastasia*. Sie erhält einen Oscar als beste
Darstellerin.

1957 Juni: Sie lernt den schwedischen
Theaterproduzenten Lars Schmidt kennen.
November: Sie trennt sich von Roberto Rossellini.

1958 *Indiscreet* (*Indiskret*). Die Ehe mit Rossellini
wird annulliert, weil die Heirat vor Bergmans
Scheidung erfolgt war und damit ungesetzlich ist.
21. Dezember: Sie heiratet Lars Schmidt in London.
The Inn of the Sixth Happiness (*Die Herberge zur
6. Glückseligkeit*).

1959 Ein französisches Gericht spricht ihr das
Sorgerecht für die drei Kinder von Rossellini zu.
Der Vater weigert sich, Unterhalt zu zahlen.

1964 *Der Besuch*.

1974 *Murder on the Orient Express* (*Mord im
Orientexpress*). Sie erhält einen Oscar als beste
Nebendarstellerin.

1978 *Höstsonaten* (*Herbstsonate*). Nominierung
für einen Oscar.

29. August 1982 Sie stirbt an Krebs.

CHRONOLOGIE

29 août 1915 Ingrid Bergman naît à Stockholm de Justus et Friedel Adler Bergman. Son père tient une boutique de photographe.

1918 La mère d'Ingrid succombe à une maladie du foie.

1927 Son père meurt d'un cancer de l'estomac. Ingrid est recueillie par sa tante Ellen, qui décède six mois plus tard. À l'école, Ingrid joue dans des pièces de théâtre.

1931 Travaille comme figurante chez Svensk Filmindustri.

1933 Est admise au Théâtre royal dramatique de Stockholm.

1934 Apparaît dans la comédie *Le Comte de Munkbro* ; décroche un contrat chez Svensk Filmindustri.

10 juillet 1937 Épouse le Dr Petter Lindstrom.

20 septembre 1938 Naissance de sa fille Pia.

1939 Signe un contrat avec David O. Selznick en février. *Intermezzo*.

1941 *Dr. Jekyll et Mr. Hyde*.

1942 *Casablanca*.

1943 *Pour qui sonne le glas*. Sélectionnée aux Oscars.

1944 *Hantise*. Remporte l'oscar de la Meilleure actrice.

1945 *Les Cloches de Sainte-Marie*. Sélectionnée aux Oscars. *La Maison du docteur Edwardes*.

1946 *Les Enchaînés*.

1948 *Jeanne d'Arc*. Sélectionnée aux Oscars.

1949 Tournage de *Stromboli* en Italie avec Roberto Rossellini. En juin, elle découvre qu'elle est enceinte de lui. Le 5 août, elle annonce son intention de divorcer de Petter Lindstrom et de quitter Hollywood. Le 6 août, elle annonce sa grossesse.

1950 2 février : naissance de Robertino Rossellini. 19 avril : partage des biens avec Petter Lindstrom, qui obtient la garde de Pia. 24 mai : mariage à Rome avec Roberto Rossellini.
1er novembre : divorce de Petter Lindstrom aux États-Unis.

1952 Naissance de ses jumelles Isabella et Isotta.

1954 *Voyage en Italie*.

1956 *Anastasia*. Remporte l'oscar de la Meilleure actrice.

1957 Juin : rencontre Lars Schmidt, producteur de théâtre suédois. Novembre : se sépare de Roberto Rossellini.

1958 *Indiscret*. Son mariage avec Rossellini est invalidé. 21 décembre : épouse Lars Schmidt à Londres. *L'Auberge du sixième bonheur*.

1959 Un tribunal français lui confie la garde des trois enfants qu'elle a eus avec Rossellini. Ce dernier refuse de lui verser des pensions alimentaires.

1964 *La Rancune*.

1974 *Le Crime de l'Orient-Express*. Remporte l'oscar du Meilleur second rôle féminin.

1978 *Sonate d'automne*. Sélectionnée aux Oscars.

29 août 1982 Décède d'un cancer.

PORTRAIT (1946)

Coming in 1949
JOAN OF ARC
starring
INGRID
BERGMAN
in COLOR by
TECHNICOLOR

4

FILMOGRAPHY

FILMOGRAFIE

FILMOGRAPHIE

Landskamp (1932)
Girl in queue (unnamed)/Mädchen in der Warteschlange (ungenannt)/jeune fille en train de faire la queue (non créditée).
Director/Regie/réalisation: Gunnar Skoglund.

Munkbrogreven (eng. 'The Count of the Monk's Bridge', fr. Le Comte de Munkbro, 1934)
Elsa Edlund. Director/Regie/réalisation: Edvin Adolphson, Sigurd Wallen.

Bränningar (eng. 'Ocean Breakers', 1935)
Karin Ingman. Director/Regie/réalisation: Ivar Johansson.

Swedenhielms (eng. 'The Family Swedenhielms', fr. La Famille Swedenhielm, 1935)
Astrid. Director/Regie/réalisation: Gustaf Molander.

Valborgsmässoafton (eng. 'Walpurgis Night', dt. Walpurgisnacht [aka Die Sünde wider das Leben], fr. La Nuit de la Saint-Jean, 1935)
Lena Bergström (Johan's secretary/Johans Sekretärin/secrétaire de Johan).
Director/Regie/réalisation: Gustav Edgren.

På solsidan (eng. 'On the Sunny Side', fr. Du côté du soleil, 1936)
Eva Bergh. Director/Regie/réalisation: Gustaf Molander.

Intermezzo (1936)
Anita Hoffman. Director/Regie/réalisation: Gustaf Molander.

Dollar (1938)
Julia Balzar. Director/Regie/réalisation: Gustaf Molander.

En kvinnas ansikte (eng. 'A Woman's Face', dt. Das Gesicht einer Frau, fr. Visage de femme, 1938)
Anna Holm (aka/alias Anna Paulsson).
Director/Regie/réalisation: Gustaf Molander.

The Four Companions (dt. Die vier Gesellen, fr. Les Quatre Camarades, 1938)
Marianne. Director/Regie/réalisation: Carl Froelich.

En enda natt (eng. 'Only One Night', fr. Une seule Nuit, 1939)
Eva Beckman. Director/Regie/réalisation: Gustaf Molander.

Intermezzo (eng. aka 'Intermezzo: A Love Story', 1939)
Anita Hoffman. Director/Regie/réalisation: Gregory Ratoff.

Juninatten (eng. 'A Night in June', fr. Nuit de juin, 1940)
Kerstin Norbäck/Sara Nordanå.
Director/Regie/réalisation: Per Lindberg.

Adam Had Four Sons (dt. Adam hat vier Söhne, fr. La Famille Stoddard, 1941)
Emilie Gallatin. Director/Regie/réalisation: Gregory Ratoff.

Rage in Heaven (dt. Gefährliche Liebe, fr. La Proie du mort, 1941)
Stella Bergen Monrell. Director/Regie/réalisation: W. S. Van Dyke II.

Dr. Jekyll and Mr. Hyde (dt. *Arzt und Dämon*, fr. *Dr. Jekyll et Mr. Hyde*, 1941)
Ivy Peterson. Director/Regie/réalisation: Victor Fleming.

Casablanca (1942)
Ilsa Lund. Director/Regie/réalisation: Michael Curtiz.

For Whom the Bell Tolls (dt. *Wem die Stunde schlägt*, fr. *Pour qui sonne le glas*, 1943)
María. Director/Regie/réalisation: Sam Wood.

Gaslight (dt. *Das Haus der Lady Alquist*, fr. *Hantise*, 1944)
Paula Alquist Anton. Director/Regie/réalisation: George Cukor.

Saratoga Trunk (dt. *Spiel mit dem Schicksal* [aka *Die Intrigantin von Saratoga/Abrechnung in Saratoga*], fr. *L'Intrigante de Saratoga*, 1945)
Clio Dulaine. Director/Regie/réalisation: Sam Wood.

The Bells of St. Mary's (dt. *Die Glocken von St. Marien*, fr. *Les Cloches de Sainte-Marie*, 1945)
Sister Mary Benedict/Schwester Mary Benedict/

Sœur Mary Benedict. Director/Regie/réalisation: Leo McCarey.

Spellbound (dt. *Ich kämpfe um dich*, fr. *La Maison du docteur Edwardes*, 1945)
Dr. Constance Petersen.
Director/Regie/réalisation: Alfred Hitchcock.

Notorious (dt. *Berüchtigt* [aka *Weißes Gift*], fr. *Les Enchaînés*, 1946)
Alicia Huberman Sebastian.
Director/Regie/réalisation: Alfred Hitchcock.

Arch of Triumph (dt. *Triumphbogen*, fr. *Arc de triomphe*, 1948)
Joan Madou. Director/Regie/réalisation: Lewis Milestone.

Joan of Arc (dt. *Johanna von Orléans*, fr. *Jeanne d'Arc*, 1948)
Joan of Arc/Heilige Johanna von Orléans/Jeanne d'Arc. Director/Regie/réalisation: Victor Fleming.

Under Capricorn (dt. *Sklavin des Herzens*, fr. *Les Amants du Capricorne*, 1949)
Lady Henrietta Flusky. Director/Regie/réalisation: Alfred Hitchcock.

Stromboli (1950)
Karin. Director/Regie/réalisation: Roberto Rossellini.

Europa '51 (eng. 'The Greatest Love', dt. *Europe 51*, 1951)
Irene Girard. Director/Regie/réalisation: Roberto Rossellini.

Siamo donne (eng. 'We, the Women', dt. *Wir Frauen*, fr. *Nous les femmes*, 1953)
As herself/als sie selbst/dans son propre rôle.

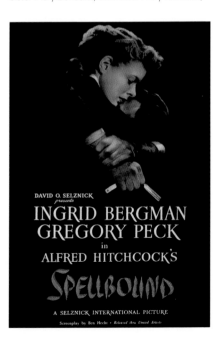

'The Chicken' segment/Episode «Ingrid Bergman»/épisode «Ingrid Bergman». Director/Regie/réalisation: Roberto Rossellini.

Giovanna d'Arco al rogo (eng. 'Joan at the Stake', fr. *Jeanne au bûcher*, 1953)
Giovanna d'Arco (Joan of Arc)/Heilige Johanna von Orléans/Jeanne d'Arc. Director/Regie/réalisation: Roberto Rossellini.

Viaggio in Italia (eng. 'Journey to Italy', dt. *Reise in Italien* [aka *Liebe ist stärker*], fr. *Voyage en Italie*, 1954)
Katherine Joyce. Director/Regie/réalisation: Roberto Rossellini.

La Paura (eng. 'Fear', dt. *Angst*, fr. *La Peur*, 1955)
Irene Wagner. Director/Regie/réalisation: Roberto Rossellini.

Anastasia (1956)
Anna Koreff/Anastasia. Director/Regie/réalisation: Anatole Litvak.

Elena et les hommes (eng. 'Paris Does Strange Things' [aka 'Elena and Her Men'], dt. *Weiße Margeriten*, 1956)
Elena Sokorowska. Director/Regie/réalisation: Jean Renoir.

Indiscreet (dt. *Indiskret*, fr. *Indiscret*, 1958)
Anna Kalman. Director/Regie/réalisation: Stanley Donen.

The Inn of the Sixth Happiness (dt. *Die Herberge zur 6. Glückseligkeit*, fr. *L'Auberge du sixième bonheur*, 1958)
Gladys Aylward (aka/alias Jan-Ai). Director/Regie/réalisation: Mark Robson.

Goodbye Again (dt. *Lieben Sie Brahms?*, fr. *Aimez-vous Brahms ?*, 1961)
Paula Tessier. Director/Regie/réalisation: Anatole Litvak.

The Visit (dt. *Der Besuch*, fr. *La Rancune*, 1964)
Karla Zachanassian. Director/Regie/réalisation: Bernhard Wicki.

The Yellow Rolls-Royce (dt. *Der gelbe Rolls-Royce*, fr. *La Rolls-Royce jaune*, 1965)
Gerda Millett. Director/Regie/réalisation: Anthony Asquith.

Stimulantia (1967)
Mathilde Hartman. 'The Necklace' segment/Episode „Smycket" („Das Geschmeide")/sketch «Le Bijou». Director/Regie/réalisation: Gustaf Molander.

Cactus Flower (dt. *Die Kaktusblüte*, fr. *Fleur de cactus*, 1969)
Stephanie Dickinson. Director/Regie/réalisation: Gene Saks.

A Walk in the Spring Rain (dt. *Die Frau des Anderen*, fr. *Pluie de printemps*, 1970)
Libby Meredith. Director/Regie/réalisation: Guy Green.

From the Mixed-Up Files of Mrs. Basil E. Frankweiler (dt. *Claudia und das Geheimnis des Engels*, 1973)
Mrs. Frankweiler. Director/Regie/réalisation: Fielder Cook.

Murder on the Orient Express (dt. *Mord im Orient-express*, fr. *Le Crime de l'Orient-Express*, 1974)
Greta Ohlsson. Director/Regie/réalisation: Sidney Lumet.

A Matter of Time (dt. *Nina – Nur eine Frage der Zeit*, fr. *Nina*, 1976)
Countess Sanziani/Gräfin Sanziani/Comtesse Sanziani. Director/Regie/réalisation: Vincente Minnelli.

Höstsonaten (eng. 'Autumn Sonata', dt. *Herbstsonate*, fr. *Sonate d'automne*, 1978)
Charlotte Andergast. Director/Regie/réalisation: Ingmar Bergman.

A Woman Called Golda (TV) (dt./fr. *Golda Meir*, 1982)
Golda Meir. Director/Regie/réalisateur: Alan Gibson.

BIBLIOGRAPHY

Bergman, Ingrid with Burgess, Alan: *Ingrid Bergman: My Story.* Delacorte, 1980.

Boccardi, Luciana: *Dossier Ingrid Bergman: Una Vita per il Cinema.* Venice, 1983.

Brown, Curtis: *Ingrid Bergman.* Galahad, 1973.

Leamer, Laurence: *As Time Goes By.* Harper & Row, 1986.

Meyer-Stabley, Bertrand: *La véritable Ingrid Bergman.* Pygmalion, 2002.

Steele, Joseph Henry: *Ingrid Bergman: An Intimate Portrait.* Delacorte, 1959.

Taylor, John Russell: *Ingrid Bergman.* St. Martin's, 1983.

IMPRINT

© 2007 TASCHEN GmbH
Hohenzollernring 53, D-50672 Köln
www.taschen.com

Editor/Picture Research/Layout: Paul Duncan/Wordsmith Solutions
Editorial Coordination: Martin Holz, Cologne
Production Coordination: Nadia Najm and Horst Neuzner, Cologne
German Translation: Thomas J. Kinne, Nauheim
French Translation: Anne Le Bot, Paris
Multilingual Production: www.arnaudbriand.com, Paris
Typeface Design: Sense/Net, Andy Disl and Birgit Reber, Cologne

Printed in Italy
ISBN: 978-3-8228-2208-1

To stay informed about upcoming TASCHEN titles, please request our magazine at www.taschen.com/magazine or write to TASCHEN, Hohenzollernring 53, D-50672 Cologne, Germany, contact@taschen.com, Fax: +49-221-254919. We will be happy to send you a free copy of our magazine which is filled with information about all of our books.